Away Went the Farmer's Hat

by Jane Belk Moncure
illustrated by Terri Super

Published by

Mankato, Minnesota

Grolier Books is a division of
Grolier Enterprises, Inc.,
Danbury, CT.

The Library —
A Magic Castle

Come to the magic castle
When you are growing tall.
Rows upon rows of Word Windows
Line every single wall.
They reach up high,
As high as the sky,
And you want to open them all.
For every time you open one,
A new adventure has begun.

Mandy opens a
Word Window.

Guess what she reads?

A farmer was in his field one day.
The wind blew the farmer's hat off
his head. Away went the hat . . .

up and around and

d
o
w
n

on a
horse's
head.

"What a fine hat," the horse said.

The  horse wore the hat,

but not for long. The wind blew the
hat off his head too. The hat went . . .

up and around

and

d
o
w
n

on a
pig's head.

"What a fine hat," the pig said.

The pig wore the hat, but not for long.

The wind blew the hat off her head . . .

up and

around

and

down

on a
cow's
head.

"What a fine hat," the cow said.

The cow wore the hat,

but not for long. The wind blew
the hat off her head and . . .

up

and around

and

d
o
w
n

on a
goat's head.

"What a fine hat," the goat said.

13

The goat wore the hat, but not for long.

The wind blew the hat off her head.

The hat went up  and around and
down to a stream.

"What a fine boat," a little duck said.

15

The duck floated along in the hat . . .

until she came to a waterfall.
Down went the hat . . .

down
and
around

and into the high grass.

A rabbit came by. "My, what a fine
nest for my babies," said Rabbit.

The baby rabbits stayed in the
farmer's hat, but not for long.

They hopped away,
one by one . . .

until the hat was empty.

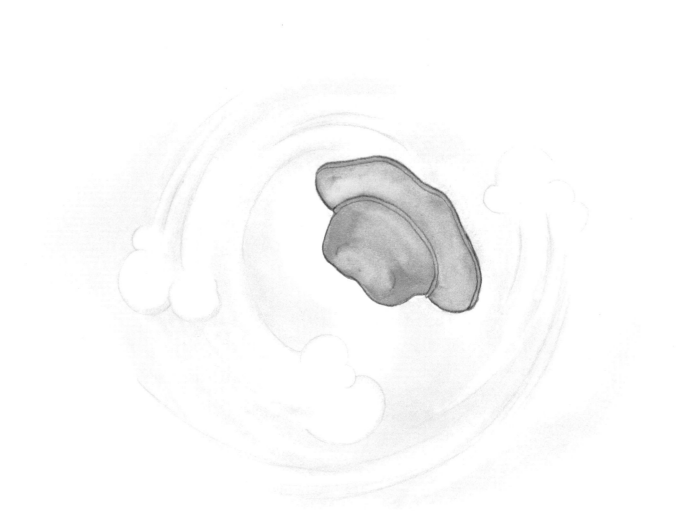

Then the wind blew the hat
into the air and . . .

up  and around
and
down.

Just then a
bird flew by.
"My," said the bird.
"What a fine nest
for my baby birds."

The baby birds stayed in the farmer's hat, but not for long.

One by one, they flew away.

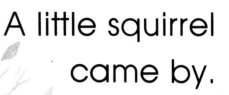

A little squirrel
came by.

"My, what a fine
nest for my baby
squirrels," she said.

The baby squirrels stayed in the
farmer's hat, but not for long.

One by one . . .

they climbed out of
the hat and ran down
the tree.

Now the hat was empty. And all
the leaves were off the trees and . . .

who came riding by,
but the farmer
on his horse.

"My hat in a tree?
How can that be?"
asked the farmer.

He pulled it down and held it
on his head all the way home.

His wife tied two strings to his hat.
"These," she said, "will keep the hat
on your head where it belongs."